*To Jone & A*

*Live Your Dreams* yvy

# The 7 Racing

# Rules

How to Win in Business and in Life

By Alex Alley and Paula Reid

An environmentally friendly book printed and bound in England by
www.printondemand-worldwide.com

**Mixed Sources**
Product group from well-managed
forests, and other controlled sources
www.fsc.org  Cert no. TT-COC-002641
© 1996 Forest Stewardship Council

**FSC**

PEFC Certified
This product is
from sustainably
managed forests
and controlled
sources
www.pefc.org

**PEFC**
PEFC/16-33-415

This book is made entirely of chain-of-custody materials

# Contents

# Foreword by Hamish Taylor

**M**ISSION/VISION, GOALS, STRATEGY, PLANS, Budgets, Customer Promises, Skills, Measures, Processes – the subjects of much internal debate and countless books and training courses. However, a major concern for me is that they are all basic building blocks that should be in place for our organisations before our 'race' even starts. Moreover, if you assume that our competitors will also have these basic pieces in place from the start, then it must be how we behave during the race that will ultimately give our teams the edge over the competition.

In the world of Alex and Paula, the goal was clear from the start (to win the race!) as were the critical strategies, skills etc. Therefore, they concentrate their attention on giving us a series of practical guidelines to ensure we can conduct the race to the best of our ability after the starting gun has fired.

If these 7 rules can work for Alex and Paula in the extreme circumstances they have encountered, they can certainly work for the rest of us:-

How often do personal or departmental agendas get in the way of delivering *'best for boat'*?

How much time is wasted in debating issues that are not part of our *'controllables'*?

We plan contingencies for major disruptions (especially where health and safety are concerned) but what about day-to-day (more likely and frequent) issues like *'MOB'*?

Have we provided enough clarity of direction such that, if asked, all staff would identify the same ultimate goal (*'Two watches, one boat'*)?

Are we close enough to our teams to ensure that, in times of stress, we will see attitudes come to the fore such as *'Race not retire'*, *'Choose your attitude'* and *'Pain is temporary'*?

In business, we live in a seemingly endless cycle of strategy, planning and budget reviews. This book is, for me, a very refreshing and useful reminder that success in business is about how you then deliver these plans on a day-to-day basis.

### *Master Thief*

A few years ago, the Inspired Leaders Network used the title 'Master Thief' to describe my work with projects that take ideas from one environment to use in another (beds in aeroplanes using a yacht designer, Disney principles for airport queuing, rugby referees for Risk and Compliance management etc). I believe firmly that, if you want a breakthrough, you must look outside your current environment! I first worked with Alex and Paula when we were involved with the London Organising Committee of the Olympic Games in sharing lessons from Olympic sports that could be applied to business leadership. What better place to look for inspiration in your own business, workplace or personal 'race' than from those who have raced in some of the most extreme environmental conditions on the planet?

Alex and Paula may not be able to write your strategy and plans for you, but they can certainly provide you with practical tools and advice to help you deliver them – bigger, better and faster!

**Hamish Taylor – 'Master Thief'**

Former CEO Eurostar, CEO Sainsbury's Bank, Head of Brands British Airways.

# Preface

THERE HAVE BEEN COUNTLESS BOOKS written about better management, better leadership, self help, discovering a better you... We've certainly read our fair share of them and although they are thought-provoking, we have discovered that they rarely reveal brand new content - ideas or suggestions that are unexpectedly innovative or original.

When reading these books, how often do you find yourself agreeing with them without thinking? The answers are familiar because the tips are common sense; deep down we know what we should be doing to get ahead.

So *why* are people still reading this type of book? And why hasn't everyone succeeded already?

We believe that the advice these books impart is usually very laudable, but over a period of time it gets forgotten or misplaced and invariably people revert to their old ways with the same inevitable results – do what you always do and you will get what you always get.

So the challenges are to firstly *retain* this valuable advice and then *do* something about it. To properly engage with the passive text so that the best bits – the bits that you really want to change for the better and do something about, become part of you – embedded in your attitudes, behaviours and skills.

What we have done with **The 7 Racing Rules** is to firstly give each rule a 'hook', a remarkable and inspiring story to hang it on, helping to bring the principle to life in the mind's eye so that it becomes memorable. Our seven *racing* rules were inspired from competing in the Global Challenge Round-the-World yacht race. They are born from real, win-or-lose situations. So each rule is named and delivered using yacht racing terminology and extreme scenarios to bring them to life and to help embed them in the memory banks.

Secondly, these rules should be regarded as 'habits' for achieving *winning performance*. They are not just rules for reading about, not even rules for thinking about, but are rules about taking the time and effort to develop the attitudes, behaviours and skills for achieving winning performance in you, your team and your organisation.

Our aim is to develop and inspire in you:

Winning attitude / mentality first, which leads to →

Winning behaviours, which lead to →

Winning skills / processes, which lead to →

Winning results, which lead to →

Winning lessons & learning (through reviews), which lead to →

Winning habits = self-perpetuating.

So, yes, these rules are hooked into remarkable and inspirational examples to help you to remember them, but they are also backed up with performance coaching, training, facilitation, e-learning, speeches and workshops if you want support to help embed them so they become self-perpetuating winning habits.

It's your choice. At the end of the day, only you can change you.

*There is only one thing stopping you from achieving your goals and that one thing is YOU. If you are determined enough to succeed, then you will.*

www.velocitymadegood.co.uk.

*Combining extreme sailing experience with business expertise to create winning performance development that is unique, powerful and deep rooted.*

# Introduction

**A**LEX ALLEY AND PAULA REID crewed in the Global Challenge Round-the-World Yacht Race. They were core crew on the same boat, sailing the whole distance of 36,000 miles in ten months. Their boat – *Team Stelmar* – finished 6<sup>th</sup> out of a fleet of 12; an amazing achievement considering they undertook two separate medical evacuations in the Southern Ocean and twice had to divert to Cape Horn (once to Puerto Williams and once to Ushuaia). These two separate incidents cost *Team Stelmar* an additional 13 days at sea as they sailed an extra 3000 miles.

Additionally, *Team Stelmar* won the most 24-hour distance trophies and are the outright speed record holders for the race – 276 miles in 24 hours. They also won the leg from Boston to La Rochelle and came 3<sup>rd</sup> from Sydney to Cape Town.

Alex and Paula knew they were on the best boat because they experienced more than the rest of the fleet; the highest highs and the lowest lows with their medical emergencies and podium places. They learned a lot. They learned fast. Their learning curve was as steep and challenging as the 50' waves they climbed in the Southern Ocean. They learned about teamwork, leadership, resilience, motivation and crisis management. They learned it in such a way that they will never forget. They learned big lessons in a tough environment. They learned deep lessons which don't come often in a lifetime.

Since the race, they have been sharing their inspiration, tips and lessons with hundreds of organisations, including commercial corporations, charities, NGOs, government departments, professional bodies, schools, academies, individuals and professional sports teams, who have all benefited from Alex and Paula's experience.

Through their inspirational talks, interactive workshops, leadership development programmes and experiential learning, Alex and Paula have refined their messages, had many opportunities to mesh their metaphors more thoroughly between sailing and business, incorporated feedback and received hundreds of positive testimonials about their unique, memorable and involving approach.

Their USP lies in their genuine ability to combine their inspirational experience with business expertise to create powerful, unique and deep-rooted leadership and performance development[1].

In distilling their original book – *BOAT to BOARDROOM* – they have further developed seven core principles, which have been named **The 7 Racing Rules**. These are seven key lessons for winning in business and in life. These seven principles are held by the authors to have the greatest impact of all the tips and lessons they have shared with 1000s of people since returning from the Global Challenge.

---

[1] www.velocitymadegood.co.uk

# The Global Challenge

AFTER TAKING AN INEXPERIENCED TEAM of paratroopers around the world in the 1973 Whitbread Round-the-World yacht race, Sir Chay Blyth originated the Global Challenge concept – taking ordinary people and putting them into teams to compete in a global ocean race. If they had the right mental attitude and physical ability, the sailing skill could be taught.

The Global Challenge was conceived in the late eighties; a race like no other. It first ran in 1992 as the British Steel Challenge. In 1996 and 2000 it ran as the BT Global Challenge. Then in 2004 it became known simply as the Global Challenge. 12 teams were selected from some 5000 initial applicants and were allocated identical 72' steel racing yachts. Everything about the yachts was the same; the only difference was the crew. Drawn from all walks of life, from company directors to students, everyone had to raise the £26,750 needed to enter and also be able to take a year off.

In October 2004 the race started from Portsmouth and raced around the world in seven legs with stops in Buenos Aires, Wellington, Sydney, Cape Town, Boston and La Rochelle before returning to the finish in Portsmouth some 30,000 miles and 10 months later.

Alex and Paula were among the crew onboard the yacht sponsored by a Greek shipping company called *Stelmar*, owned by Stelios Haji-Ioannou (Easy Jet).

During the course of the race, *Team Stelmar* had to deal with Man Overboard, medical evacuations, storms, freezing temperatures, gear failure, waterspouts and becalming. They were at sea racing for 184 days and on one leg alone were at sea for eight weeks. They covered 34,599 miles and, as well as being on the podium twice, they set several records including the outright 24 hour distance record for the race.

They lost and they won, but they learned.

# Analogy

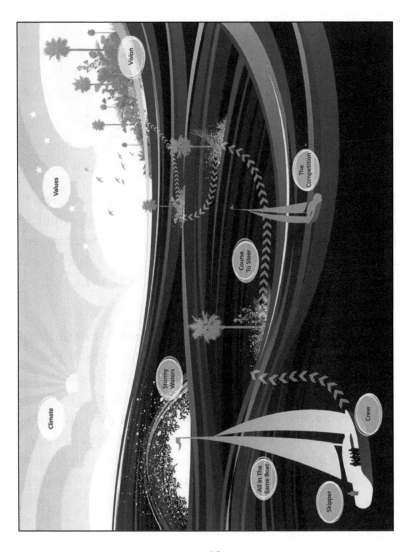

O N REVIEWING THE RACE and returning to work, Alex and Paula observed how much symmetry there was between racing the yacht and running a business. The headlines of this analogy are as follows:

Firstly we are *'all in the same boat'*. Literally in sailing terms on the yacht, but in business everyone ultimately works for the same organisation and thus experiences the same conditions at the same time while working towards the same goals.

There is someone ultimately in charge – ultimately responsible – someone with whom the 'buck stops'; the *skipper* or the CEO.

There may also be several layers of leadership and management within an organisation, sharing the leadership load with the skipper: partaking in decision making; communication; performance management; strategic thinking; financial and operational management and so on. On the boat we had the *Navigator* and *Watch Leaders.*

On an ocean-racing yacht there are usually two *watches*, working separately in shifts but with the same goal – to win. Collectively they make up the *crew* or staff. These people are crucial to the daily running of the boat or organisation; inching it towards the ultimate realisation of success. The two watches on the boat represent different departments, teams, shifts or locations of a business – working separately on a day-to-day basis, but together in contributing towards long-term business goals.

Next is the *'vision'* - the ultimate destination - the tropical island paradise; the winner's podium; the 1st place trophy; the finishing line.

Our vision was to be on the top step of the winner's podium at the end of the race, receiving the winner's trophy in front of a standing ovation of cheering supporters and admiring competitors – we held this strong, vivid picture in our minds all the time to focus and drive us with determination, resilience and courage.

Your vision should be the extremely successful and ambitious place you are heading towards. The vision should be positive, inspirational and aspirational. It needs to drive decision making and behaviours; motivate and focus everyone on board. It should be a vivid, compelling picture of the perfect, successful future.

In order to reach the vision - the finishing line - we need to navigate our way there and have a *'course to steer'* or a strategic plan determining the preferred route among the many options available. On the way to the final destination, we set ourselves smaller goals or landmarks to pass. Each of them needs to be successfully completed if we are to reach our finishing line.

*'Competition'* is never far away. Certainly as we were racing around the world against 11 identical yachts, there were times when we were very close indeed, even after several weeks in the vast expanse of the ocean. We could either physically see our competition or would receive performance updates four times a

day with progress statistics for all 12 yachts. Knowing your competition keeps you focussed, but you shouldn't spend too much effort worrying about what they are up to; you can't change their performance but you can change your own. We had a rule to keep our 'eyes on the boat' and concentrate on how our performance could give us that edge over them.

In life, business and certainly in yacht racing there will be times that are tough – *stormy waters*. They should be expected and planned for because no matter how optimistic you are, there *will* be difficult and challenging times ahead.

When sailing, the long-term *climate* and short-term *weather conditions* have a massive bearing on our performance, especially as we rely on the wind to move. We cannot do anything to change it but we must deal with its effects. The same is true in business. International businesses may be affected by global conditions and mega trends such as the financial climate, which affect everyone – including the competition. So the winner will be the organisation that has the better strategy and performance because of their *forecasting* ability; their ability to *read the weather* and then their ability to correctly conclude what the implications are – to them, their business and the marketplace.

Finally there are the *guiding stars* by which we navigate; our values which we live by. On the race yacht in the Global Challenge our values were simple and easy to remember – Safe, Happy and Fast – and they shone the way for us.

# Sailing Comparisons

| | | |
|---|---|---|
| The Boat | = | The organisation |
| Skipper | = | MD/CEO/Owner |
| Navigator | = | Strategic leader |
| Watch Leaders | = | Managers/leaders |
| Watch Teams | = | Divisions, departments, teams |
| Core Crew | = | Permanent full time employees |
| Leggers | = | Temporary full time employees |
| Watch system | = | Shifts |
| RORC[2] | = | Business regulators |
| The Ocean | = | Marketplace |
| Climate | = | Long term business climate |
| Weather | = | Local conditions |
| Stormy waters | = | Tough times |
| Man Overboard | = | Crisis |
| Southern Ocean | = | Very tough operating environment |
| | | |
| Competitors | = | Competitors |
| Waypoints | = | Goals or deadlines |
| Velocity Made Good | = | Most efficient progress in the right direction |

---

[2] Royal Ocean Racing Club

# The Rules

#1 Best for Boat

#2 Control the Controllables

#3 Practise your MOB

#4 Race not Retire

#5 Two Watches, One Boat

#6 Choose your Attitude

#7 Pain is Temporary, Pride is Forever

# #1 Best for Boat

**W**E KNEW THAT TIMES WOULD get tough during the race.

Picture the scene; you are deep in the Southern Ocean, 56° south, it is past one o'clock in the morning and you have been on deck for the last three hours sailing the boat. There is a dusting of snow on the deck from earlier. It is an effort to keep up your concentration and stay awake and impossible to keep warm in the freezing conditions. Every few minutes an icy wave crashes over you, taking your breath away and sometimes sending you sprawling along the deck. You have already been at sea for two weeks and have not seen another boat for five days. There are still over three weeks racing before the finish of the leg. On checking the time you see there is only half an hour to go before watch change and the chance to go below deck, out of the cold, grab a hot drink and burrow down in your fleece-lined arctic sleeping bag.

However, the wind eases and a sail change is needed to maximise the performance of the boat. The task itself is a challenging one. Carrying the heavy, 100kg, wet, frozen sail up to the bow of the boat is a four-man job in itself. Then unzipping the frozen bag with numb fingers and clipping it onto the metal forestay, ready to hoist. Next, dropping the existing sail, dragging that back and folding it into its bag before stowing it away on deck. All of this in the dark, on a pitching deck while being pounded by the icy waves.

Another glance at your watch tells you there are now only 20 minutes left of your time on deck. What do you do? The easy option would be to leave the sail change for the other watch, BUT that would mean sailing below optimum for those 20 minutes plus the 20 minutes needed to perform the change, so 40 minutes in total underperforming.

The right thing to do is to change the sail there and then, even if it means working beyond your watch finish time to see the job through. This is where the *Best for Boat* rule kicks in. It's about making the right decisions at the right time; doing the right job that is best for boat.

At the end of this particular leg of the race, three boats finished within one and a half minutes of each other – after 40 days of racing, day and night! Competition is always close, even if you can't see it, and a small performance gain over a short time can make a significant difference to the end result.

Whenever we were faced with this type of situation or decision, we asked ourselves, 'What is *Best for Boat*?' The answer usually came easily and quickly. Human feelings and thoughts about the job are slow and cumbersome to analyse, whereas best for boat gives us an incisive and immediate performance evaluation tool.

Another example: When we arrived into port at the end of each leg, everyone would be looking forward to a well-earned break from the race. However, we weren't there on holiday; we were there to race around the world and *Best for Boat* meant we should stay and get *Stelmar* race-fit for the next leg and not spend all our port time on holiday.

We had a vision – to be first, and we were not going to realise that vision unless we strived for it. So the *Best for Boat* decision was to forgo much of our time off and work on the boat, preparing for the next leg. This was our own free time we were giving up, but we knew that if we wanted to make the boat go faster, that's what we had to do.

A third example of the *Best for Boat* rule is having the right people on the boat and in the right roles. There needs to be a helmsman to steer the boat and trimmers to control the main sail and headsails. Then grinders who wind the winches and someone to look at the sails and 'call' the trim to the grinders so they can be pulled in or let out to maximise efficiency. There are also foredeck crew who change the sails and crew at the mast who help with this. Just behind the mast is the 'snakepit' where 23 control lines are led. The people here need to liaise with all the others to make sure things run smoothly – they are the communicators. Finally, there is the navigator who decides the best route and the skipper who is ultimately responsible.

Lots of people doing different jobs, but each one critical to the proper and efficient working of the boat. Each role is very specific and certain people will naturally be better at some jobs than others. Some roles are more high profile, but they are all just as important. It is about having the right people in the right place doing the right thing at the right time.

On *Stelmar*, there were people who were better at some jobs than others. Take helming for instance. It is easy to steer a boat – rather like driving a car with a large steering wheel – however, it is an acquired skill to drive the boat effectively and get the maximum speed out of it all the time. Even though everyone was equally committed to the team, had the same rights and generally enjoyed helming, it was decided that only certain people would be allowed to helm while we were racing. Some people would initially be de-motivated by this, but knew it was in the best interest of the team – *Best for Boat*. They would be part of a winning boat with the right leadership and a winning mindset. This would inevitably reap rewards – ideally podium places but at least just the knowledge that they gave a once-in-a-lifetime opportunity 100% effort.

Another example: at critical times, such as the start of each leg when the boats were close to each other in confined waters, we decided to have the best specialists from the entire crew doing their job on deck, rather than choosing just one watch. This meant we had the ultimate team working at critical moments, even though it couldn't be sustained for the entire race. Because of this, *Stelmar* was first across the line in five out of the seven race starts – having the best people in the right jobs paid off.

With every decision we made, every action we took, we asked ourselves, 'Is this the best decision/action for the boat?' 'Will it make the boat go faster?' Asking these simple questions took away the emotion and made the decision-making process much easier, faster and more effective.

If you keep doing the same thing, then you will keep getting the same results. If you want to change the output, then you need to change the input.

Make sure everything you personally do is 'Best for your Boat' and you will succeed.

This core axiom can be applied within an organisation to achieve high performance and strategic effectiveness. It can easily be applied to business situations as a sharp decision-making tool.

For instance, if you are determining your organisation's strategy or restructure, having the phrase *Best for Boat* front of mind (see Case Study *p28*) as a constant reminder will clarify your decision making. You will make the right, strategically effective decisions rather than ones influenced by historical legacy, *status quo* complacency, internal politics or personal biases.

This will help you (and your team) pull away from distractions and prejudices and see the bigger picture – *objectively*. Using *Best for Boat* engenders decision making, thinking and activity that is for the greater good. If the organisation benefits from this, then the employees and customers will also benefit. The organisation will grow, prosper and survive for longer.

Of course, there will still be tough decisions to make and emotions will potentially be at variance with this principle, but *Best for Boat* takes into account the bigger picture. Some decisions will be painful – for instance, during a restructure or downsizing – but if it means that the organisation survives, then this is the more important long-term objective.

In a restructure, some people may not end up where they want to be, but *Best for Boat* is for the good of the organisation. These tough people decisions can be rationally justified; the right decisions are made for the right reasons. This is not to ignore the human element, but the 'soft stuff' comes later, after the objective thinking and *Best for Boat* decision making.

One consequence of using a *Best for Boat* approach is that it takes the emotion out of tough decision making, so that it becomes easier, clearer and quicker. History, legacy, politics, preferences and tradition are replaced with effectiveness and efficiency.

Some examples where *Best for Boat* can be applied in business are:-

- Right person, right role
- Performance management, including dismissals
- Quality control
- Use the right equipment for the job
- Taking appropriate action immediately and efficiently
- Being in a peak state for peak performance, such as rehearsing a pitch
- Devising the right strategy to achieve the business vision and mission
- Making long-term win-win decisions instead of short-term win-lose decisions

**Case Study**

*Best for Boat* can also help organisations or teams go back to the drawing board and (re)start with the right intentions.

An organisation we have worked with had their guaranteed funding taken away and suddenly found themselves in a competitive situation with very tight deadlines. The company knew they had to review their structure, strategy and budgets and seriously downsize to survive. However, they did not know where to start. 20 years had been emotionally invested in the company since it was founded by the current CEO and deputy CEO. The organisation had a 'family' culture and values and working relationships were warm, friendly and caring.

Once introduced to the *Best for Boat* principle however, the way forward for the Executive Directors became very clear.

We started from the most fundamental place; reviewing and adapting the vision, mission and values so they were (aspirationally) *Best for Boat,* fit for the new world. The organisation's strategy was then radically overhauled and became much more commercially focussed and industry-centric. The restructure was then tackled with tough determination using *Best for Boat* as the judging criteria. Rather than considering the personalities and emotions involved, the conversations and decisions were about having the right structure, job titles, roles and skills to achieve the vision, mission and strategy.

Following a series of Director and Board meetings over three months, the leadership team were justifiably proud and committed to their effective new strategy and structure.

*Then* the 'soft stuff' was implemented brilliantly by the aligned and confident leadership team as they involved and engaged their staff in best practice communication about all the changes.

Individuals affected respected and acknowledged that the right decisions had been made for the right reasons and those who stayed knew they were on a 'storm proofed' boat with excellent leadership and those who left, left with their heads held high and with positive stories to tell.

One benefit of *Best for Boat* is that everyone buys into the reasoning; shareholders, Boards of Directors, customers and employees are able to see and understand why the decisions have been made because they make strategic sense. This increases respect, integrity and loyalty, both internally and externally. The plans stack up to scrutiny, the strategy or (re)structure can be reasonably and easily explained because they have been considered objectively and decisions have been made for the right reasons. Leadership teams can then rest assured that they have done the right thing.

*'Management is about doing things right; Leadership is about doing the right things.'*[3]

---

[3] Peter Drucker

A radically different organisation was born which was fit for purpose and which had a high chance of survival.

But interestingly it wasn't just about survival any more.

The changes meant that the organisation had an exciting and innovative chance of becoming world-beating and being a shining example of how to get it right in their industry. They have since been selected to be the guiding council for the many other organisations in a similar position who are struggling to stay afloat in tough economic times.

**Rule #1 - Best for Boat**

Is everything you do, every decision you make best for your 'boat', in other words best for your organisation?

This rule is about being effective. Behaving efficiently as one team, who are all in the same boat, heading together towards future success.

This rule makes attitudes, behaviours and decision making effective, objective, clear and fast. It takes the emotion out and helps you quickly come to clear, unbiased solutions.

Questions to ask here include:

- Is *every* decision, action, behaviour and attitude in your organisation 'best for boat'?
- Will every decision, action, behaviour and attitude make your boat go faster and beat the competition?
- Are your vision, strategy, values and goals best for boat?
- Does every employee understand what best for boat is and know how to achieve it?
- Are the right people on the boat and in the right roles?
- Are decisions made quickly and easily, with clear, objective rationale?
- Is everyone, from top to bottom, striving and focused continually on best for boat?

**Is everything you do, every decision you make, Best for Boat? Use this as your judging criterion for making strategically**

effective and objective decisions, removed from bias, prejudice, legacy, politics and the norms.

Best for Boat is a Racing Rule for long term, strategic, effective and fast decision making.

This racing rule is great for sharpening your business.

# #2 Control the Controllables

I N THE EARLY DAYS of an ocean race, the boats are soon over the horizon and out of sight of the spectators. The ocean is a big place; in the Southern Ocean for instance, it is not uncommon to go for several days without seeing any other sign of life. With no other visible competitor to compare performance against, it would be easy to fall off the pace and drop back; however, it is also just as viable to keep pushing hard.

Nowadays, technology makes race viewing very easy. With the advent of satellite tracking beacons on the race boats, the organisers and spectators can follow the yachts across the oceans and watch their progress daily. However, this technology also allows the teams to monitor each other. When racing around the world in the Global Challenge, teams got a position update from the organisers every six hours.

That's like getting four performance appraisals every day.

From these positions you could work out how you were performing against the other 11 teams, looking to see if you had gained or lost miles to the competition. BUT this information had to be treated with care. It would be easy to see a gain over another yacht as an improvement in performance. Likewise a loss of miles to a competitor could be seen as a decrease in performance. But this information is not always as clear as it may at first seem.

Because the fleet would often be spread out over hundreds of miles, the conditions experienced by some were often quite different from those experienced by others. So an increase in miles gained *could* simply be due to better weather conditions, favourable local winds or currents.

A 10 mile gain may at first glance look good, but in reality if the team had pushed harder, then it perhaps could have been a 15 mile gain. Contrastingly a 10 mile loss might not be so bad in light winds, as without the team working well, it could have been a 15 mile loss.

To maintain our winning mindset and our focus on the task at hand, we would monitor our own performance continually to make sure that we were always pushing the boat as hard as we could. We had a performance chart on deck which we filled in every 15 minutes comparing our performance with previous entries. If the boat was slower and the wind had not changed, then we knew that we needed to do something to get back the pace, so set about methodically working out how to increase our speed.

We knew we had to focus consistently on our own performance 100%, no matter what the competition or the weather was doing.

**Performance below Deck**

One of the least desirable jobs on a yacht is mopping up the water that accumulates in the bilge of the boat under the floorboards. This is where the water gathers from condensation, wet clothing from crew members coming off watch, and small leaks through the deck and down the mast. Over a period of time it can accumulate quite significantly. With a racing yacht, weight is critical, and the lighter the boat, the quicker it will go, so removing this water is one way to reduce weight and hence increase performance. Pumping or mopping the bilge is one thing that we have direct control over and something that we checked every hour, removing any water that we could. Every litre adds a kilo of weight and slows us down. It may only be a tiny amount, especially relative to a 45 tonne boat, but over a long period of time, every kilo and every fraction of a knot of boat speed counts.

Every small thing that we could do - that was within our control – we did, to make the boat go faster. This management of physical performance also positively affected our performance *attitude.* If we could be 'bothered' to mop up half a kilo of water on a 45 tonne boat, then we knew we had to do anything and everything to make the boat go faster.

Similarly in business, there are various internal factors that can, if controlled, affect company performance.

The point here is that we can't control the external factors such as the weather or the competition, but we CAN control our own performance.

It is easy to blame someone or something else when things are not going well, but to truly succeed one must strive to improve one's own performance and not concentrate on the performance of others.

You have no control over the climate or the competition directly, but you do have total control over your own performance, actions and attitude so maximise those, with 100% dedication, and stop worrying about things that you have no control over. This will just distract you from the real focus – your own performance, attitude and behaviours.

*Control the Controllables* is a rule where it pays to spend time constructively looking at things you can control and work on ways to continuously improve them.

If, for instance, you feel out of control, unable to act, frustrated, overpowered or un-empowered, check whether what you are worrying about is actually within your control to affect. Classify or list your challenges or 'to do' activities under one of three headings:

1. In your control 100%
2. In an area you may be able to influence
3. Out of your control 100%

(see diagram overleaf)

If (1) above - it's 100% in your control - take action and give it your all. Be proactive and 'eat the frog'[4] or the 'elephant'[5]! Plan if you need to, but then *just do it.*

---

[4] Eat that Frog: *Great Ways to Stop Procrastinating and Get More Done in Less Time* by Brian Tracy

[5] *'How do you eat an elephant? One bite at a time'* Origin of proverb unknown

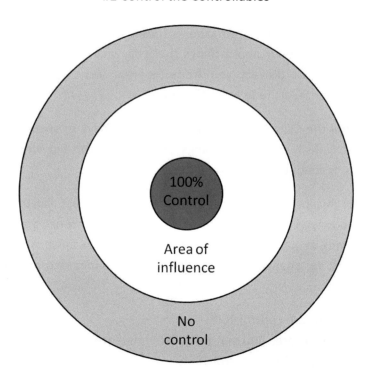

This decisiveness followed by action will give you a feeling of empowerment. Activity generates momentum and confidence. You will feel more in control and able to have an effect – you will be more effective. You will also become a role model for others, seen as someone who gets things done; someone decisive, determined and proactive who makes things happen. You will be role modelling effective decision making and action, inspiring and impressing those around you. It will give you the energy (momentum) to do more. Take control of that within your control. *Control the Controllables*.

Tony Robbins[6] refers to this as being in control of your destiny. Controlling both your *Blueprint* (your personal plan and ideas about the way your life should be) and your *Life Conditions* (the way your life is currently acted out).

Life conditions = Blueprint ⟹ ☺

Life conditions ≠ Blueprint ⟹ ☹

If your life conditions equal or exceed your blueprint, you are happy.

If your life conditions do not equal your blueprint, you are unhappy.

There are only two ways to change yourself, your level of satisfaction, fulfilment and overall happiness: change your life conditions or change your blueprint.

You have control over both of these. You decide what your personal plan is going to be – your blueprint – and you decide how to carry out your plan. If, for instance, you choose to be a highly successful sportsperson, then you will be focussed on training, nutrition, health, fitness, motor skills, etc. If you are NOT achieving this goal, then you can choose to review and change your blueprint (being a highly successful sportsperson) or your life conditions (e.g. how much training you are doing).

---

[6] Tony Robbins, American motivational speaker

It is your choice and within your control. Decisions determine your success and decisions are directly affected by your emotional state and your attitude. Decision making is an absolute power that we have, and there are three key questions to ask yourself:

1. What are you going to focus on? (something you *can* control or influence)
2. What does that positively mean? (an opportunity *not* an obstacle)
3. What are you actually going to *do*?

Similarly in coaching, the four questions are:

1. What is your goal?
2. What is your reality?
3. What are your options for getting to your goal from your reality?
4. What will you actually do?

The more you achieve, the more you will be able to achieve and your controllable area will expand (see diagram opposite).

# #2 Control the Controllables

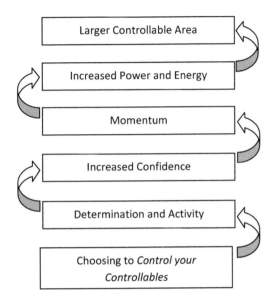

| Larger Controllable Area |
| Increased Power and Energy |
| Momentum |
| Increased Confidence |
| Determination and Activity |
| Choosing to *Control your Controllables* |

## Choose your Battles

If (2) — a task or challenge that you face is not 100% in your control and not 100% out of your control — then it is in your area of influence and in here, you should choose your battles. Choose which ones to fight and which ones to let go. How do you know which ones to fight? Use your personal judging criteria for each specific situation. Judging criteria are personal to you and the situation, but may include, for instance:

- How passionate you feel about the situation
- To what degree you think you can affect change
- Whether it is a quick win or a long campaign

- How much it supports or challenges your personal integrity, values and ethics (i.e. stand up for what you believe is right)
- Whether the timing is appropriate or opportune
- If a 'tipping point' is involved where one small action may ignite greater change

Generally, whether it is worth it on balance; whether it is worth your reputation, relationships, time and effort to fight a certain battle.

If, on consideration, using criteria such as the above, the battle is not worth fighting, then let it go. Stop worrying about it; cross it off your to-do list and forget it. Let it go physically and mentally. You will have given it due consideration and you will have made a proactive decision. This is not surrender; it is a conscious, controlled decision; know that it is acceptable to let it go and that you have chosen to do so.

If on consideration you choose to fight your battle and it's important, then you should plan your course of action in order to be best prepared. Have a strategy to increase the odds of winning: *[A strategy is] a style of thinking; a conscious and deliberate process; an intensive implementation system; the art of ensuring future success.*[7]

Strategy is the 'art of ensuring future success'. The point of having a strategy is to be best placed to win. Plan to win, don't plan for planning's sake, or because you have to.

---

[7] Sun Tzu

For instance think about:

- What do you really want? Be clear and honest about your end goal
- Work out what success looks like – is there a chance for a win: win?
- What's your bottom line? What would constitute a 'lose'?
- What are you willing to negotiate on or compromise?

Then plan your tactics; be prepared:

- Collate your evidence – first hand observations, records, facts, notes, etc
- Plan and perhaps even practise your communications
- Potentially use a mentor or positive critical person to test out your plan
- Check you are being emotionally intelligent, that you are not biased, prejudiced, being overly sensitive or emotional
- Test for 'what ifs' – what if you get response A, B or C?
- Practise answering 'killer questions' – how will you respond if you are asked X, Y or Z?
- Check the legalities if necessary, including HR
- Enter into your actions with a positive, constructive mindset
- Do your best, but you will still win some and lose some

*You can only do your best\* in the circumstances you are in, with the time and resources that you have.*

\* But do do your best!

If you don't get your desired outcome, decide whether it is worth a second (or sometimes third) push, and then let go. You have given it your best. Relegate it to the 'out of your control' area unless circumstances fundamentally change in your favour.

*N.B.* Be careful in pushing a second or third time. In business and in life, action needs to be tempered with courage, respect and maturity:

*Maturity is the balance between courage and consideration. If a person can express their feelings and convictions with courage balanced with consideration for the feelings and convictions of another person, they are mature, particularly if the issue is very important to both parties.*

*Habit 5: Seek first to understand, then to be understood.*[8]

If (3) – the situation is 100% out of your control – then stop wasting your time thinking or worrying about it and divert your efforts and attention to things you can affect, control or influence. On the boat we couldn't control what the competition did or what the weather was doing. Know about them and then control what you can control.

Have an outer awareness and then focus on the internal action – you and the boat.

Ensure that you and your boat are realising their full potential.

---

[8] Stephen R Covey, *The 7 Habits of Highly Effective People*

## #2 Control the Controllables

In business, step back and view the external world, trends and activities now and again but then focus on maximising performance internally – with you, your team and your organisation.

**Rule #2 - Control the Controllables**

When racing a yacht, much the same as in business, there are many variables that affect performance. Some we have ultimate control over – such as our own personal actions, while others we have no control over, such as the weather. This rule is about focussing your time, effort and energy on the things you can control and influence.

Questions to ask here are...

- How much time do you spend looking at or worrying about things that are actually outside of your control?
- Are there perhaps personal or political agendas wasting time and diverting your organisation's energy from its ultimate goal and future success?
- How's your time (choice) management?
- Do you know how to choose your battles within your 'area of influence'? Do you have strategies for winning these battles?
- And what can you do to increase your area of control?

**The weather was outside our control. We worked on getting the best performance from the crew and therefore the boat, whatever the weather was doing. Focus your time and energy working on what is within your control. Reduce time and energy worrying about everything else.**

**This applies to life as well as to business.**

# #3 Practise your MOB

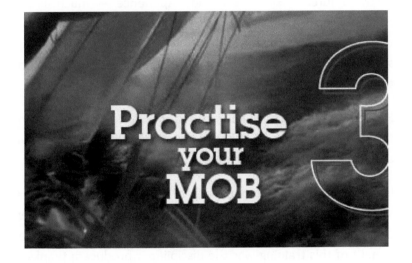

**P**REPARATION FOR A ROUND-THE-WORLD yacht race is obviously different from preparing for a business, but if you look beyond the specialist technical planning there are many similarities, and one that stands out is preparation for crises.

Training for the Global Challenge race had to be incredibly thorough; for one reason the team consisted of people with vastly different skill levels and experience – much like a company. On an ocean-racing yacht there are countless things that can go wrong – hence the phrase, 'worse things happen at sea!' Some will be more common than others and their effect on the crew and their ability to continue/survive will vary.

Having a crew member fall overboard *is* quite likely and if the MOB (Man Overboard) is not recovered quickly and efficiently, the consequences could be dire.

It was for this reason that much of our pre-race training was spent practising our MOB drill so that if/when it did happen, we all knew exactly what to do, almost without thinking. The added benefit of this training was the discipline it produced; thanks to the repeated practising, we all knew how to act in a crisis, not just a MOB situation.

In our MOB training it was important to swap the roles around so that everybody knew and understood ALL the roles and their implications. The reason for this is quite obvious – you never know who is going to go overboard! If we each had our own specialist roles for the crisis, and one person went missing, then their role wouldn't be fulfilled.

The same applies in business. It is no good giving each person a specific 'crisis management' role, because you never know what the crisis will be and who will be around to manage it. So it is important that everyone understands what needs to be done, even if that means giving each person a secondary role or a role buddy. This has the added benefit of improving teamwork, communication and cooperation between teams and employees as they understand and appreciate each other's roles.

Buddying up colleagues at work for crisis planning for example can improve:

- Teamwork
- Communication
- Co-operation between teams
- Mutual respect
- Understanding of each other's roles

**Risk Analysis**

You can plot the likelihood of something happening against its impact, as shown in the basic risk analysis diagram overleaf.

In this example, the boat sinking obviously has a huge impact but is very unlikely. MOB is much more likely and has high impact so should be expected and therefore planned for and practised.

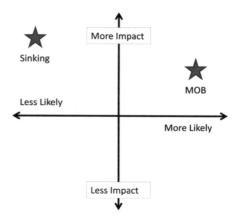

The top right segment of the grid covers what should be expected and practised most. No matter what industry you are in, or whatever you do in life, it is useful to know what to expect and what to do when things go wrong.

If you draw up your own grid and fill it with events that may happen in business, then you will have a clearer picture of what to expect and be able to prepare for it. You can score each event /10 for impact and risk to provide some basic metrics.

**No Surprises**

Anticipation is the ultimate power; being able to predict and solve problems before they happen; predicting patterns, predicting what's around the corner and being prepared. 'Forecasting' the likely weather ahead. Then, by being more in control and more proactive, teams can set themselves up to win.

They are less likely to lose someone overboard (a key staff member or client) and less likely to hit an obstacle.

It is naïve to be caught out by 'surprise' or choose to have a blind spot to a potential future failure when predictions, patterns, insights and trends can be sought, evaluated and pro-actively tackled head on.

Imagine playing a video game or racing simulator that you have never played before. You are likely to underperform on your first go. But when you have played it once, or a few times, you know what to expect and can play it better. If you practise and know what's about to happen, then you are more mentally ready and physically skilled to handle it.

**Most Likely Case Scenario**

Most organisations ask what the 'best case' or 'worst case' scenario could be. The question you really need to be asking is what 'the most likely case' scenario could be? What is your organisation's equivalent of a MOB – a high likelihood, high impact negative situation? Something that either threatens the operation, reputation or safety of your organisation or would knock you off the top spot.

It is also important to see things as they are – not necessarily better or worse. Crisis preparation requires intelligent thinking and an honest approach, which in turn requires clarity and courage.

Two questions you need to ask:

1. What is our equivalent of a MOB?
2. What will we do if/when it happens?

Some examples of business MOBs might be:

— Loss of key customer
— Competitor bringing out a cheaper or better product
— The arrival of a new competitor – more flexible and innovative
— A disruptive innovation reducing the need for your product
— Financial cutbacks
— Star employee leaving / talent drain / loss of leader (your specific equivalent of a MOB)
— Empty pipeline, product doesn't get licensed or blockbuster comes off patent

At least pro-actively recognise and tackle crisis scenarios or 'what if' events that populate the top, right-hand box of the grid – the ones which are most likely to happen and which will cause the most damage. Acknowledge them openly and give them some airtime – don't ignore the elephant in the room – get them out and talk about them. Once they are openly acknowledged, they become tangible and... tackle-able!

Then you are able to honestly and proactively  discuss solutions, communications, best practices, processes and strategies for dealing with them, or ideally prevent them from happening in the first place.

**Building Institutional Toughness**

The whole organisation can be involved in crisis scenario planning – whereby individuals and teams develop resilience and leaders demonstrate strength, courage and integrity.

Ask employees or teams for equivalents of a MOB and solutions and plans to resolve them. Create opportunities for people to detect and analyse potential future failures. ('Monitor-Evaluators'[9] or 'black-hatters'[10] would be particularly useful to invite to these exercises.) Those involved will gain a maturity – a mental toughness or resilience – through discussing and disaster planning for tough situations.

Then practise realistic scenarios. One practice is not enough and the more realistic the scenario, the more developmental it will be, producing the steadfast mental toughness when it really matters.

If the organisational equivalent of a MOB is discussed, planned and practised thoroughly, then when a crisis does happen (whatever it is), people will have the muscle memory, mental agility and situational awareness to be able to deal with it and, importantly, move on and learn from it. The more practice, the

---

[9] From Belbin's team roles. Monitor-Evaluators are great for dispassionately evaluating options and critiquing
[10] From Edward de Bono's 'Six Thinking Hats'

more discipline and resilience, and the more people will be able to cope with the crisis – any crisis – when it comes.

## Benefits of Practising MOBs

Crisis planning and practice also cultivate transferrable skills. The behaviours, skills and attitudes developed in our MOB drills, for instance, transferred easily to other similar critical situations – such as an accident on deck. Crew remained calm because they weren't thrown by the unexpected, everyone knew their roles, leadership was clear and decisive, communications were fit for purpose and teamwork was efficient and controlled.

If an organisation develops crises plans, behaviours and attitudes for its most likely/impactful crises, the plans are likely to be generally effective for other eventualities. Communications planning, role allocation, emergency procedures, continuity plans and post-crises mop-up activities are applicable across a broad spectrum of 'what if' scenarios and thus contribute to general institutional toughness, a more highly developed and mature workforce and a risk management culture.

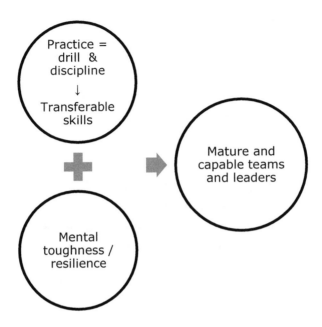

**AAR (After Action Reviews)**

Another method of mitigating risk and preparing for future eventualities – such as a MOB – is to frequently review past performance to ensure continual improvement and protection from future failure. On our boat *Team Stelmar*, we reviewed and debriefed every manoeuvre with the whole on-watch team and transferred new learning or tips to the other watch at the next watch change. We would review the whole procedure, including successes and failures, striving for peak performance through continuous learning and development. We were honest and open to self-assessment, never assuming, ignoring or diminishing the need for improvement or change.

This served as a proactive and preventative exercise. Proactively we sought continuous or disruptive innovations to improve performance, and preventatively we sought ways to protect ourselves against a potential future failure.

*One near miss could be the next MOB.*

Luck may play a part in preventing one crisis but it obviously cannot be relied upon. This is where reviews are important, even when they don't seem necessary, as some successes may be due to a specific chain of events, external factors or luck.

After Action Reviews (AARs) take place following an event or activity to discuss four key questions:

1. What did we set out to do?
2. What actually happened?
3. Why did it happen?
4. What are we going to do next time?

Lessons learnt can apply as equally to day-to-day business as to potential future MOBs.

Crisis planning sharpens the sword, enabling higher performance as well as crisis prevention and management.

It's tough staying at the top, and practising your MOB does not allow for stagnation or complacency. It does, however, bring about innovation, efficiency, resilience, teamwork, new skills, confidence and, of course, crises mitigation.

**Rule #3 - Practise your MOB**

The probability of having a crew member washed overboard in a Round-the-World yacht race is very high with a massive negative impact on the boat and the team, so it's essential to practice for this likely eventually. It would be crazy not to.

This regular practising gave us the ability not only to effectively and efficiently deal with a MOB, but also any number of other crises because the discipline, processes, behaviours and attitudes were transferable.

This rule is about crisis planning, crisis prevention and crisis management.

At some point things will go wrong or perhaps not quite go to plan.

Some questions to consider are...

- How well do you know your 'likely' worst case scenarios? What's the worst thing that could happen that is also quite probable? (These are the ones that you need to proactively do something about – you need to prepare, practise and plan for your version of a Man Overboard.)
- And if they do happen, would you know what to do and be able to deal with them? Do you have the right behaviours, skills, attitudes and processes in place?

Crises are not predictable but they should be expected and therefore planned for. Make crisis management planning part of your business planning. Have crisis focus groups working out the enhanced disciplines required in emergencies. Rehearse scenarios with various teams using different crises. Be prepared. Don't forget there are major benefits to doing this.

In life, know what may constitute a crisis in the future – a highly likely and impactful negative situation. Work out your strategy for either preventing it or mitigating the risk.

# #4 Race not Retire

*T*HE BOAT TOOK OFF ON *a particularly big wave and came crashing down. After the water rush had gone from the cockpit there was the one sound you never want to hear — especially in the Southern Ocean — 'Man Overboard!'* [11]

On the second leg of the Global Challenge race from Buenos Aires, Argentina, to Wellington, New Zealand, we had already gone from a full crew of 18 down to 16 and had one medical emergency, so this was the last thing we wanted...

While in Buenos Aires, two days before leaving, one of the crew quit and flew home. There was no time to get a replacement and we had to set off on this colossal 6,400 mile leg of the race one crew down. Not wanting to give in and to prove to ourselves and to the other teams that we could get over this, we pushed hard and gave that extra effort needed to sail the boat one person down. Within a week we were approaching Cape Horn and were in third place — a credit to our fighting spirit and determination.

But then, just a few miles short of Cape Horn, we had to stop racing and drop off another crew member for medical reasons. The detour cost us 19 hours and dropped *Stelmar* back to last place. All the hard work of the previous week was undone through no fault of our own. It would have been easy at this point to get depressed and give up (see rule #6 - *Choose your Attitude*), but we were a determined team with plenty of fight left. We were there for a reason — to race around the world and that was what we were going to do.

---

[11] Quote from *BOAT to BOARDROOM* by Alex Alley and Paula Reid

We pushed hard and very soon we had overtaken the eleventh placed boat. Within five days we had sailed past more than half of the fleet, clawing our way up to 5$^{th}$ place, and in the process set the 24 hour distance record for that leg of the race – all with two crew missing. Had we given up we would not have had the satisfaction and pride of achieving that.

It was at this point in the race that we had our second medical situation. This time it was much more serious. 1,000 miles deep in the Southern Ocean, outside help was days away. One of the crew had been hit by a huge wave and thrown into the rigging, sustaining a very serious fracture of his arm. It was called as a 'Man Overboard' as all crew were immediately needed to deal with the emergency. We had to get him to help as quickly as we could, however that would still take us five days. Tim was strapped in his bunk and pumped full of morphine to ease the pain until we could get him stable and into medical care. Eventually we reached Ushuaia back in Argentina and Tim was flown straight to Buenos Aires for surgery.

Back on board we still had to get the boat to the finish of the leg in Wellington and then prepare for the next leg of the race to Sydney. We were now three crew down and 2,000 miles behind the rest of the fleet, with no chance of catching them before the end of the leg as they now had less than 1,000 miles to go to the finish.

The Southern Ocean is a desolate, empty expanse of freezing water. Storms gather in intensity from west to east regularly with no land mass to stop them. We would be heading out alone without the 'safety net' of the other eleven race boats should something else go wrong. The race organisers strongly suggested that we retire from that leg of the race and use our engine. They wanted us to head north to a latitude of around 40° south and then motor to New Zealand as quickly as possible. The reason for this advice was because at that latitude there are commercial shipping and aircraft routes, so should another emergency occur, help would be a little closer than it would be further south in the Southern Ocean.

However for us to take this route, it would mean retiring from this leg of the race and taking a one place penalty, effectively finishing in 13th place out of 12 boats and losing an extra point. The other option was to return to the spot where the accident occurred and restart racing; finishing in 12th place and therefore saving a point.

We all knew that we couldn't expect any more than 12th place, but we were there to 'race' and not cruise. Our pride was at stake and we were determined to prove once again to ourselves and to everybody else that we could do it. After a discussion amongst all of the crew, it was unanimously decided to ignore the race organisers' advice. We headed back to the Southern Ocean to continue racing. Five days later we reached the position of the accident and notified the race committee that we were racing again. Only this time we were racing against the clock to get to the finish and have enough time to prepare for the next leg.

It was tough; really tough. It was freezing cold, with the very real and ever present danger of being swept overboard into the icy waters. Despite being alone, out of radio contact and far behind the rest of the fleet we kept pushing the boat as hard as we could.

Eventually we made it to Wellington and were greeted with a heroes' welcome – we had done it, against the odds. The other teams had all gone away for a break and their boats had been stripped down and lifted out of the water – we were the only boat in the marina, but the whole town turned out to welcome us in.

It was now that we discovered what had happened to one of the other boats.

One of the other teams had also suffered a serious medical emergency. A crew member had become very sick and needed to be taken to hospital as quickly as possible. Luckily for them however, they were no longer in the middle of the Southern Ocean, and within helicopter range of the Chatham Islands. They headed north to rendezvous with the helicopter and the sick crewman was lifted off and flown straight to hospital for treatment. This detour cost the team a matter of hours and they were now only one crew member down. However, with only a few days to go, having already sailed for over a month, they decided to retire and motor sail the remaining few hundred miles to the finish.

For them it meant a frustrated and dejected team; for us it meant that we were no longer last. We saved two points by not retiring and coming in 11$^{th}$ (Rule #2 – *Control the Controllables*), even though the odds were well and truly against us. We will forever have the pride that we DID race around the world and we never gave up.

**Never Give Up**

*Race not Retire* characterises unremitting resilience and determination (especially) against the odds. On climbing Everest, Sir Edmund Hilary noted:

*...because of strong motivation, you keep plugging on and you seem to be going okay and nothing seems to be going wrong, so you persist. And we persisted, of course, and ultimately, set foot on the summit.*

*Race not Retire* calls upon progress where every inch counts, every action, every day, every watch; taking small steps, one by one; never giving up until you reach your goal. Immense achievements can be realised just one step at a time... climbing Everest, sailing 36,000 miles around the world, leading a business successfully for years and years. If the end goal was the only focus, then most people wouldn't even take the first step. The end goal will motivate and drive people to be forward looking, but the next single step ensures action. When times are especially tough – seemingly impossible, then the long term vision has to play second fiddle to basic survival. Surviving one hour at a time or getting through the next watch:

*When you think you are running on empty, there will generally be a little more fuel left in the tank for when you really need it... don't look at the big picture: it's the small steps you grind out one by one that get you there.* [12]

We sailed around the world, mile by mile, watch by watch. We persevered with courage and resolve and we never gave up – not even after our second medical evacuation in the Southern Ocean.

*Anyone can give up; it's the easiest thing in the world to do. But to hold it together when everyone else would understand if you fell apart, that's true strength.* [13]

In the Global Challenge there were certainly times when everyone else would have understood if we'd retired from Leg 2 of the race. Circumstances were heavily stacked against us and many people either suggested or expected us to retire. Sir Chay Blyth [14] even strongly advocated retirement.

But we didn't.

We didn't give up, we didn't retire, we raced on.

Not only did we earn two extra points which were crucial to the overall race leader board, but we also felt huge pride in our attitude.

---

[12] Team Stelmar's sponsor
[13] Source unknown
[14] Originator and Director of the Global Challenge business

Would Sir Chay Blyth have given up? Did he give up when he sailed solo around the world the wrong way or rowed across the Atlantic with John Ridgway? No! When you are the one in the thick of it, it is your decision to give up or not. Interested parties on the sidelines do not feel the same feelings or experience the same experience. Bystanders may encourage you to give up because it looks too much, too dangerous, too risky, from their point of view – but don't. It's *your* challenge, *your* adventure, *your* pride that is at stake. And when you are in the thick of it and your blood is up, your courage can be screwed to the sticking place and you can dig deep into that amazing inner well of resolve and determination.

It is amazing what you can achieve when you try. How many times have you looked back and thought, 'wow, I did that'?!

Never give up...

... because you never know what may happen and you will be able to take pride and satisfaction in your fortitude. Pain is temporary, but pride is forever:

*...sometimes you're ahead, sometimes you're behind... the race is long, and in the end, it's only with yourself.*[15]

You will gain strength from your strength. This then gives you something to hold on to and motivate you internally, when you are up against it or when the odds aren't in your favour. Every inch counts...

---

[15] Sunscreen song, Baz Luhrmann

You will also know that you gave it your all and you can't do any more than that.

The alternative of course, is to give up. To surrender in defeat.

*Don't Quit;*
*Don't quit when the tide is lowest,*
*For it's just about to turn.*
*Don't quit over doubts and questions,*
*For there's something you may learn.*
*Don't quit when the night is darkest,*
*For it's just a while to dawn.*
*Don't quit when you've run the farthest,*
*For the race is almost won.*
*Don't quit when the hill is steepest,*
*For your goal is almost nigh.*
*Don't quit for you're not a failure,*
*Until you fail to try.* [16]

And if you give up on the long journey, you will never get to your destination. You don't even have a chance. What if you gave up too soon *when the tide was about to turn*? One more step, one more effort could have made all the difference. The end of the race is the time to stop and then to refocus your energies into something new – but not before.

If you truly have a winning attitude, then never give up, whether you are first, last or somewhere in the middle.

Give 100% commitment to you and your boat while you remain in the race.

---

[16] Jill Wolf

**Rule #4 – Race not Retire**

It's a long, tough race – not just for us all the way around the world, but also in business and in life, and you need to keep pushing for progress and performance, inch by inch, day by day.

You are in it for the long run.

You need to somehow keep racing, and never give up, whatever happens. Never drop off the pace.

This rule is about continually striving for peak performance.

- So do you and your team – your whole organisation – have a winning attitude? Focussed constantly on success and peak performance?
- Can you continue with a racing attitude when times are tough?
- Are you strong enough to break through the pain and keep racing?

This is about continually aiming for that top spot.

...continually having a winning attitude.

...continually going for it, with absolute 100% conviction and belief that you are doing the right thing.

...having a racing attitude with every action, activity, and tactic, every employee and every customer... always racing, always winning and striving to be the best.

It's a long, tough race. Keep pushing inch by inch. You never know what you are capable of, what's round the corner or what may happen to the competition.

# #5 Two Watches, One Boat

**R**ACING A YACHT AROUND THE WORLD is a 24 hours a day, 7 days a week operation, with no down time. The more time you spend actively sailing the boat (compared to letting it sail on auto pilot), the better the performance will be. On long, single-handed races this is quite obviously impossible to achieve and the performance of the boat is compromised while the skipper is asleep. However, with a full crew to share the load the boat can be kept powering along 24 hours a day, maintaining continuous high performance.

This is achieved is by splitting the crew into watches, usually two. While one watch is on deck racing the boat, the other is below deck resting, and they rotate on a regular basis (typically every four or six hours).

Within this system there needs to be a balance of expertise on both watches with each person having a double or opposite number on the other watch, sharing the same tasks.

On our boat we had a two watch system of eight people in each watch with the Skipper (CEO) and Navigator (Senior Strategic Leader) outside the watch system. It was crucial to have a balanced mix of skills, experience and attitudes to maximise the day-to-day performance of the boat consistently – it was a long race.

During a watch changeover – five times a day – there was a handover between opposite numbers to inform the upcoming crew about what had been happening, what to expect and to share best practices. This way the oncoming watch was up to speed much more quickly and therefore performance continued at a higher rate without faltering. (Rule #1: *Best for Boat.*)

From a safety point of view it was also important to let the new watch (new shift) know the situation they were picking up and what weather (local conditions) to expect in the near future. There should be no surprises for the joining crew (who were asleep less than 30 minutes before coming on deck).

On handovers, teams should share:

- What's happened – useful headlines
- What to expect – facts and gut feel
- Best practice, tips and learnings

At one point during the race, in an attempt to improve the overall performance, it was decided to have a competition to see which watch could sail the most miles over a number of days. The intention was for each watch to push as hard as they could for the sake of the one boat.

However, the idea backfired. Each watch, comprising very competitive people, started to keep information, communication and motivation to themselves, rather than share it with the other watch. So rather than having two teams working together for the greater good, we ended up with two teams competing against each other to the detriment of each other and ultimately the entire team.

Very quickly this practice was scrapped as we were all in the same boat, working towards the same goal. It was important that each watch shared information and best practice with their opposite number in order to maximise the performance of the whole team. At the end of the day we were not competing amongst ourselves but against the other eleven boats in the fleet, so the better we worked *as one team*, the better the overall result would be and the more likely we were to beat the competition.

The effort and focus was concentrated on everyone working together to beat the external competitors – the other boats (organisations) we were racing against – eradicating any internal competitiveness between watches (such as departmental incentives or silo'd attitudes).

In organisations, 'Two Watches, One Boat' translates as two – or more – teams working collaboratively towards the same end (vision, mission, strategy, goal, project, etc.). This is further described as follows:

Two watches: different departments, offices, regions, countries, teams, shifts, projects, etc.

One Boat: as in you are all in the same boat (organisation). All in the same boat implies that everyone is experiencing the same general working conditions at the same time and are working towards the same end. People who are all in the same boat must work as a team because they face the same challenges and need to cooperate in order to succeed. The boat (organisation) will achieve greater progress if the teams share the effort and share the passion for reaching the destination.

*So, how do you lead teams so that the different 'watches' are working collaboratively towards the progress of the 'one boat'?*

1. Share the destination.

Sharing the destination is ultimately about sharing the vision. The vision needs to be compelling, ambitious, aspirational, exciting, inspiring – visionary. Teams should understand exactly what their vision looks like in the long term, why they have it and how it translates tactically and locally.

Our vision on the Global Challenge race was to come first. To be on the top step of the winner's podium at the final awards ceremony in Portsmouth, in front of a standing ovation of the other crews, friends, family, sponsors and press. The vision was colourful, detailed, multi-sensory and motivational. Organisational visions should be equally exciting and compelling, driving and aligning everyone towards a successful future point.

2. Share the mission or raison d'être.

We also shared the same mission; the same raison d'être. Ours was 'to *race* around the world' – not to cruise or sail or swim or rally – but *race*. We were very clear on that point. We existed as a team because we had all signed up to a Round-the-World yacht *race*; our raison d'être was therefore to race and win. This was a very important point when, on Leg 2, we had to decide whether to *race or retire (Rule #4)* after our second medivac.

3. Share the strategy and goals.

Organisations also need to share the strategy in order to operate as *One Boat*. The leadership team or Senior Management Team may have determined the strategy but it still needs to be thoroughly and clearly shared with everyone on the boat to ensure alignment and empowerment.

4. Share the values.

Finally, *Two Watches, One Boat* requires alignment around the culture and values. Behaviours and attitudes need to be consensual; the values respected, lived and believed in; the culture tacitly understood and adhered to.

When values, vision, mission, goals and strategy aren't shared, then teams/departments may conflict or become silo'd, perhaps even working against each other to the detriment of the overall performance. When teams get too competitive or incentive systems are unfair, then collaboration takes second place to competition. If there is divisiveness around fundamental principles, such as whether the strategy is about price or quality, then potentially the company divides or people leave to set up their own company – and thus create two boats.

Here are some ways to achieve collaboration between teams to benefit the one organisation:

- Everyone shares, understands and buys in to the five unifying essentials at the heart of the organisation: the vision; mission; values; strategy; and goals. All of these should be clear; communicated effectively and repeatedly. An example in our case was that our skipper literally talked through the Navigational Charts at the start of each leg with both watches on deck. He explained the geography, our route, our strategy for winning – why we were taking the course we were taking and what conditions to expect. Leaders should do the same at the start of each business period – gathering their crew to explain the chosen route and strategy for the next leg of the race.

—   Leaders communicate the why and the what (vision, mission, strategy), employees involved in the how (values, tactics). Once the skipper and navigator shared their vision and strategy for each leg, it was then delegated to each watch to carry out the strategy on a daily tactical basis through behaviours appropriate to our values – safe, happy, fast. This sharing of the work and sharing of responsibility helps to engender a *One Boat* culture with less barriers and divisiveness vertically or horizontally across the structure.

—   Leaders and managers walk the talk, actively demonstrating collaboration, *One Boat* mentality and behaviours. On *Team Stelmar* both the skipper and navigator kept out of the watch system so that they remained balanced across the two watches; ensuring that both teams held the same understanding and knowledge and were assuredly working in the same direction. Leadership was not biased or localised, and so remained objective and focussed on the bigger picture.

— The induction programme, ongoing development, performance management and appraisals affirm and support the *One Boat* principle. *Team Stelmar*'s leggers (new crew who joined the boat for each leg) were given a thorough induction, enabling them to feel comfortably and intrinsically part of the *one team* as soon as possible, no matter which watch they were assigned to.

— Genuine collaboration between teams — not superficial. Cross-team, department, function, country and project working. Our two watches developed slightly different ways of working, had unique systems and practices, developed their own stories and jokes, but when it came to the work that really mattered, the collaboration was *Best for Boat (Rule #1)* This was in the main part achieved through watch handovers at every watch change, 'happy hour' every Sunday at 6pm (which meant that both watches were on deck together for one hour to share stories and discuss team issues) and in port debriefs with the whole crew to review the past leg and seek performance improvements for the next. These Global Challenge activities are easily transferrable into business: quality handovers, 'happy hours' and whole team debriefs.

**Alignment**

**Two Watches, Two Boats**

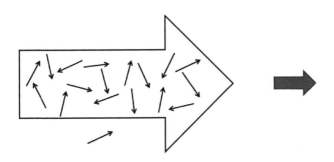

This diagram represents unaligned individuals and teams, not working collaboratively, and so pulling in different directions, potentially in conflict with each other or potentially working outside the organisation's strategy/brand, producing counter-productive wasted efforts. Activity is visible, but not necessarily the right activity at the right speed in the right direction *(Velocity Made Good).*

The CEO/MD/Board (represented by the larger arrow) is working too far ahead or too far away and is not in touch with the reality of the organisation. They are not close enough to their crew to drive and share direction. They are too far removed to notice or be able to influence the disorder behind them.

## Two Watches, One Boat

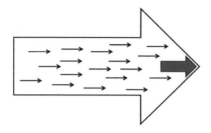

Aligned leadership team with a clear and visionary direction, shared by management and employees. There are no resisting forces creating friction. Individuals and teams are pulling in the same direction, thus creating momentum and increasing efficiency, speed and effectiveness (maximum *Velocity Made Good*).

The CEO/MD/Board are leading from the front – being visionary and future proofing – but are also visible, accessible and in touch with the crew. Leadership is forward-looking with long-term macro vision, but also close enough to be able to focus on internal detail and productivity. Balancing both is key. Zooming out and zooming in.

**Rule #5 Two Watches, One Boat**

Ocean racing requires two watches to work collaboratively together, 24 hours a day. Without this collaboration performance is impaired. An easy trap to fall into is where the two watches don't work effectively together, they don't share knowledge or best practices, and may be so busy competing against each other, they lose sight of the common enemy – the other boats they are racing against.

Your organisation may well contain separate teams and departments, regions, locations, countries, shifts, functions.

They should be collaborating, connected, glued together - vertically and horizontally - all working for the sake of the one boat.

Facing the same direction and pulling together.

Striving for the same goals.

Having the same priorities.

Moving together towards the same shared vision, mission, strategy, values, goals.

Ultimately you are not competing against each other internally; this is destructive and takes the focus and energy away from beating the real competition.

Questions...

- Are all your departments and teams working cohesively and effectively together, sharing information and best practices with each other?
- Is everyone in your organisation pulling in the same direction, towards the same goals, with the same priorities?
- Is there smooth collaboration – genuine trust and respect between teams?
- Or do you have people working in silos, teams competing against each other, maybe even sniping between departments, rivalry, confused priorities or bad press?
- Essentially, could teamwork across your organisation be improved?

**Your organisation may well consist of different teams, departments, locations, countries, shifts. Prevent them from turning into silos. Work on connecting them; glueing them together into 'one team / one boat'.**

# #6 Choose your Attitude

H AVING RACED OVER 5000 MILES down the length of the Atlantic Ocean on Leg 1, *Team Stelmar* was performing well as a team. Everyone knew their roles and responsibilities and got on sufficiently well with each other to perform competently in the race.

As the team were preparing for the second leg of the race, from Buenos Aires to Wellington, thoughts were on the daunting task that lay ahead. Racing down the east coast of South America the temperature would fall and the winds would increase.

Cape Horn is the gateway into the Southern Ocean and once around this point there is nothing to check the force of the waves and the wind. The storms build and continue to circle around the globe with nothing standing in their way. This is the reason that the Southern Ocean is so violent and daunting and why Cape Horn is so notoriously dangerous.

During the preparations for this leg, one of the *Stelmar* crew decided he couldn't face the challenges ahead and left the race. With only two days to go before the re-start we couldn't get a replacement and had to leave for the hardest and longest leg one crew short. We were certainly disappointed but we couldn't do anything about it and had to make the best of it and move on – we chose our attitude.

By focusing on the race and not the absent team member, we reached Cape Horn one week later in third place and challenging for the lead.

BUT one of the leggers had been ill since the start of the leg and we didn't know what was wrong with her or how serious it was. We had to make a decision – head out into the Southern Ocean and hope things didn't get any worse or stop racing and drop her off.

It was difficult at the time to accept the only real decision – suspend racing and get her to proper medical attention. We surrendered our strong third place and headed for the nearest port in Chile; Puerto Williams. We were there for only 20 minutes and as she headed off in an ambulance we returned to racing, now two crew down. That detour cost us 19 hours and we were now last. By the time we rounded Cape Horn, the leaders were 200 miles ahead. Again we made a conscious decision not to be despondent or angry, and focussed on a new goal – not to be the last boat into Wellington. We re-shuffled the watches around and made sure we had the right mix of skills and experience on each – *Best for Boat*.

By directing our energy and being positive, within 24 hours we had indeed caught and passed the eleventh placed boat. Five days later we were less than 50 miles from the leader and were battling for fourth place. We had caught and passed over half the fleet and in doing so set the 24 hour record for that leg of the race. To others following the race we were an inspiration. We didn't accept our handicap of two missing crew. By re-focussing and getting on with it, we were able to overcome the difficulties ahead of us – we chose our attitude.

However, our situation was about to change; much for the worse. Early on the morning of 13<sup>th</sup> December, one of the crew was hit by a huge wave and shattered his upper arm. We were 1,000 miles out in the Southern Ocean, battling with freezing temperatures and massive waves. Having done so well in working our way through the fleet, we were once again faced with a decision. There was no chance of rescue from a passing ship – there simply aren't any in the Southern Ocean. We were also out of range for a helicopter and it would have been too rough and too dangerous to attempt an air-sea rescue.

So once again we had to suspend racing and turn back to South America – to Ushuaia in Argentina this time. Wellington was simply too far to sail with a crew member so badly injured. It would take us five days to get to Ushuaia, sailing in completely the opposite direction, past the boats we had worked so hard to overtake.

**Choose your Attitude**

When we were over 1,000 miles from land and civilisation and things went so wrong, the natural response would have been to blame someone or something else. We could have wallowed in self-pity and allowed ourselves the luxury of getting depressed (and bring the rest of the team down too) – we deserved better!

It is all too easy to shift blame rather than take responsibility and *do something about it*. In the middle of the Southern Ocean nobody else is going to help, so we have a decision to make;

either get depressed and blame others, or deal with it. One will get the team down; the other will find a solution.

You can be constructive and positive and re-motivated by a crisis, or negative, despondent and finger-pointing. One makes the team pick up and you feel better, one doesn't. One has energy for moving on, one doesn't. It is your choice and yours alone as to which attitude you adopt.

It is easy, however, to follow peers and join in when they are shifting the blame – but will this solve the problem/issue? Of course not; it makes it much harder to find the solution. What it takes is someone to change their attitude to a positive one and then positively affect those around them. One rotten apple in a barrel may turn the others sour. Equally if one charismatic individual can demonstrate a positive attitude – especially in a negative situation – others can choose to follow their lead.

Surround yourself with positive people. If your colleagues or peer group tend to moan and complain, then perhaps it is time to change them or you may struggle to succeed. Positive people attract more positive people and *get things done*, not because they are more clever or capable, but because they choose to have a positive attitude.

How many successful, motivated people do you hear moaning? None. That is because they have chosen their attitude – a positive one.

You can choose yours...

After our experience in the Southern Ocean, we had certainly earned the right to feel depressed and begin to blame others, but we chose not to.

It's not the situation that really matters; it's your response to it that counts. Negative things happen – unforeseen, uncontrollable, unwanted – and you can choose to behave predictably and typically with negative emotions and attitude, or you can choose to take the more positive route with a positive mindset.

*'What doesn't kill you makes you stronger.'*

This is about human nature; distinctively we have emotional responses to good and bad news. But over time and with practice you can talk yourself or retrain yourself into a positive state. The more often you do this, the easier and more habitual it becomes.

The benefits are – you feel better, and your positive attitude will positively affect others.

*'In every crisis there is opportunity'* – look below at some of the heartfelt and extraordinary responses we received on the boat when we decided to *race not retire* and *chose our attitude* after our second medical evacuation in the Southern Ocean. This is the sort of impact you can have on others when you are inspirational with your positive attitude:

*As to 'you lot' I think you once again showed fantastic will power and determination in turning around so quickly, especially when you all must be pretty knackered and emotionally drained and so my respect for you remains even greater than before.* [17]

*Team Stelmar are an inspiration to anyone who is thinking of doing this race and the determination should be an example to us all.* [18]

*It was fantastic news that you are to continue racing. In view of the sheer determination, grit and courage you have all shown so far, to do anything other than continue with the race would have been unthinkable. You are an amazing team.* [19]

*Every hard time they face, can only bring new strength and determination... and prove once more that Team Stelmar are something pretty special.* [20]

*I am just in awe of what Team Stelmar are doing right now.*

*To Team Stelmar: well done, a huge decision and one that none of you will ever regret. Admiration all round from us back at home.*

*These people are extraordinary and deserve our admiration. What they do afterwards will surely benefit not only themselves but all they come into contact with.*

*You guys have gone through more than anywhere near a fair share of trouble. But you have survived and handled it so well!*

---

[17] Andrew Roberts, Project Director, Global Challenge

[18] Simon, supporter

[19] Mother of a crew member

[20] Skipper's sister

*You are the real winners of this leg; my hat is off to your difficult decisions, fantastic team effort and almost inhuman fighting spirit.* [21]

*At Stelmar (the organisation) we're all immensely proud of your resolve and resilience...* [22]

*There is a raft of people out there all cheering and willing you on. What a tale you will have to tell.* [23]

---

[21] Rival skipper
[22] Stelmar sponsors
[23] Sir Chay Blyth

**Rule #6 - Choose your Attitude**

In any situation – in business and in life – you can choose your attitude.

You can be constructive, positive and motivated or you can be destructive, negative and demotivated!

One attitude has positive energy for moving on and learning, leading to greater performance and the other can be destructive – on you and others – and result in a decrease in performance.

- Do you have an engaging, constructive and energetic culture throughout your whole organisation?
- Does everyone exhibit a 'can-do' attitude?
- If there is a challenge or crisis, do you or your team react positively with enthusiasm and solutions?

*Choose your Attitude.* **You can be constructive, positive and re-motivated by a crisis, or negative, despondent and finger-pointing. One makes the organisation pick up and you feel better, one doesn't. One has energy for moving on, one doesn't. No blame. Debrief, learn and move on. A mistake is only a mistake if no-one learns from it.**

# #7 Pain is Temporary, Pride is Forever

**H**EADING BACK TO USHUAIA IN ARGENTINA, just north of Cape Horn, with a seriously injured crew member onboard was disheartening for everyone. We had embarked just two months earlier to race around the world in the World's Toughest Yacht Race and it was certainly living up to its name. We had just set the 24 hour record, even though we were already two crew down and had fought our way back up from last place after one medical evacuation which meant turning around 180° and sailing back past the boats we had worked so hard to overtake.

During the five days it took to reach land and get our casualty off the boat for medical attention, we were deciding what to do next. We were still on the second leg of our Round-the-World race, albeit 2,000 miles behind the rest of the fleet. Ultimately we still had to get the boat to Wellington to rejoin the others and continue in the race.

The race organisers were putting a lot of pressure on us to retire from the leg and motor-sail to Wellington at a latitude of around 40° South in order to be within range of other shipping if we needed assistance. If we did this, then we would have to take a one point penalty for retiring.

Our vision right from the start was to 'race' around the world, not just sail around – an important difference. During the five days sailing back to Ushuaia we talked amongst ourselves as to what we should do. There were mixed feelings at this point; the Southern Ocean is a formidable place and some people understandably didn't want to spend more time there than necessary.

When we arrived in Ushuaia there was an ambulance waiting to take Tim to hospital to have his arm operated on. There was also another ambulance for a couple of the other crew who had some more minor injuries. One of them was Paul who needed a hydrocortisone injection in his elbow to relieve his pain. As we were going to be in port for a few hours to re-provision the boat, Paul took the opportunity to call his wife back in the UK. He said he was going to fly home to spend Christmas with his family. The chance to see them for Christmas versus heading back to the freezing storms for another month at sea was a tempting option. But his wife had other ideas...

She reminded him how much he had been looking forward to and preparing for this race and said that he would regret leaving the team at this point. She told him he had to stay on the boat and fulfil his dream. She was right of course.

She then cancelled his credit cards so that he couldn't get a flight home!

Paul returned to the boat with the resignation that he would continue and not go home for Christmas. It was the best decision he ever made.

It was certainly tough heading back out and continuing to race rather than retire (rule #4), but Paul and the rest of the team gave it their all to reach Wellington before their deadline of 21st January.

When *Stelmar* did eventually cross the finish line just before midnight on the 20th, the team were ecstatic; they had achieved something amazing which they could be truly proud of. Not only had they raced through the Southern Ocean, and effectively completed two medivacs with no outside assistance, but because they had decided not to retire, they were awarded 11th place due to another boat retiring just a couple of days from the finish.

It's not what happens, but your response to it that counts.

Life and business are not always plain sailing with fair winds – it would be rather dull if it was! We all enjoy 'highs' – racy, fast, exhilarating sailing, or more comfortable times, perhaps moored up safely in a marina with a bottle of wine, but we also experience lows and tough times – doldrums or storms, tornados, rough seas, heavy going, Southern Ocean medivacs.

It is easy to be good when it's good. It's when times are tough it really counts.

*Commitment starts when the fun stops.*[24]

Successful people do tough things. It's during difficult times that you can really show what you are made of – stronger stuff – and it's during difficult times that you learn and grow the most. If you behave with courage and integrity, you can draw strength from your fortitude and therefore be able to dig even deeper. In other words, just knowing that you are behaving in such a way

---

[24] Robyn Benincasa, Adventure Racer

as to make you feel proud feeds your sense of satisfaction and self-fulfilment and creates even more positive motivation for you to draw strength from.

Other people will also draw strength from you; you will be a point of reference, a role model standing out in contrast to others who let go, give in, get depressed, angry, or run away and hide.

In sport *Pain is Temporary, Pride is Forever* is a frequently used phrase to motivate athletes to push themselves beyond the pain barrier and achieve greater heights, distances and speeds. The 'pain' is often physical but it can be emotional or psychological too.

Lance Armstrong, having survived cancer and won the Tour de France seven times, uses a different version of the phrase but to similar effect:

*... the fact is that I wouldn't have won even a single Tour de France without the lesson of illness. Pain is temporary. It may last a minute, or an hour, or a day, or a year, but eventually it will subside and something else will take its place. If I quit, however, it will last forever.*[25]

In life the 'pain' may be physical or emotional, or brought about by a situation such as divorce or redundancy. This would typically involve a period of angst, depression or anger. Firstly, one can choose one's attitude, and secondly, know that *Pain is*

---

[25] Lance Armstrong, Every Second Counts

*Temporary, Pride is Forever.* The pain will not last forever, but the pride will. During difficult, painful times, it would be best if one behaved with integrity, respect and dignity, and therefore be able to hold one's head high with pride.

In business, the 'pain' may be a leadership battle, restructure or hostile takeover. Again, it is easy — and usually expected — to behave in a negative manner in these situations, but the best behaviour — *Best for Boat* and best for self — is to behave professionally; with wisdom, maturity and courageous integrity.

Don't lower yourself to the expected norm. Behave in a manner that will allow you to hold your head high and allow others to learn from you.

Step up and do the right thing... you know that you can.

**Rule #7 - Pain is Temporary, Pride is Forever**

Two medical evacuations in the Southern ocean within one week, was hard for us to deal with. However, knowing that we gave it our best – responding with integrity, courage and commitment – will be with us forever.

- So when there is any sort of pain in your organisation, are the attitudes and behaviours professional, respectful, mature and considerate?
- Do the reactions exemplify courage and integrity?
- Is there pride and belief in your products / services, outcomes / outputs, in yourself, in your team, in the organisation?
- Also, do you encourage pride during and after projects and activities?
- Celebrate success?
- Recognise exemplary work despite the conditions or even despite the outcomes? (Because of course, you can have a failure – or pain - which is outside of your control – even though everyone has given it their best shot...)

There will be times when there is pain. In your personal or professional life.

At work there may be pain through people leaving, competitor successes, poor sales, reduced income, mergers or takeovers...

But the way you behave in these times will always stay with you.

Pain is temporary, but pride will last forever.

**Behave always in a way that will make you proud - for always. Even if you are tired, or in pain, or just lacking the energy, these things are temporary. Your memory of how you behaved will last forever.**

# About the Authors

## *Alex Alley*

Alex is a highly competitive individual who, after teaching himself to sail as a child, turned professional at 19 and went on to become world champion at 20. His sailing experience now amounts to over 100,000 miles. He is still very much involved with offshore racing and is regularly asked to speak and inspire delegates at conferences about his racing experiences and run leadership development programmes.

Alex is a co-founder and Director of **Velocity Made Good** and runs workshops helping companies become more focussed on winning with **The 7 Racing Rules**.

## *Paula Reid*

Paula applied to do the Global Challenge four months before the race started and got her place confirmed with *Team Stelmar* two months later. She hadn't sailed before.

Paula believes in living life to the full and has already achieved over 95 things on her 'bucket list' of things to do. Achievements include: sailing around the world; winter mountaineering on Mont Blanc; walking on hot coals; paddling the Mekong; walking across the country; running the marathon and kayaking the length of the Thames. She has also competed in the World Bog Snorkelling Championships!

Her philosophies are to 'live life to the full' and 'just do it'.

She is a speaker, trainer, consultant, facilitator and coach specialising in Leadership; helping leaders to become visionary, inspirational, courageous, effective and innovative. Paula is also a Director of **Velocity Made Good**.

# Velocity Made Good Ltd

VMG combines extreme sailing stories and analogies with business expertise to create leadership and performance development that is unique, powerful and deep rooted.

VMG delivers inspirational talks, interactive workshops, books and online learning on the following four themes:

1. The Big Picture
   *Vision, Mission, Values, Strategy, Goals.*
2. The 7 Racing Rules
   *How to win in business.*
3. Stormy Waters
   *Leading and managing in difficult times.*
4. Boat to Boardroom
   *Specific solutions for leaders, managers and teams.*

www.velocitymadegood.co.uk

# BOAT to BOARDROOM

Alex and Paula's first book *BOAT to BOARDROOM* has inspired teams the world over.

It comprises two books in one: the complete story of *Team Stelmar* in their race around the world followed by business chapters on Leadership, Teamwork, Strategy & Tactics, Personal Development, Crisis Management, High Performance, Motivation and Communication.

*"A leadership book that reads like an adventure story."*
Gary Dyer, Team Leader, Unum

*"Alex and Paula transport us to Cape Horn and the wildest ocean of the world for a fresh look at leadership and teamwork in real life situations."*
Simon MacDowall, Director of Comms and Marketing, HMRC

*"A gripping story with powerful lessons; a fascinating and useful book."*
Mike Rotherham, PhD, Performance Consultant

*"Alex and Paula take you through the remarkable story of 'Stelmar' - their leg from Buenos Aires to Wellington is the stuff of legend - and relate their experiences to broader application in everyday life and business in a very practical way... The section on advanced teamwork is spot on."*
M. Blore, an Amazon reader